W9-BVJ-038

BINDI
Irwin

by Golriz Golkar

CAPSTONE PRESS

a capstone imprint

Bright Idea Books are published by Capstone Press
1710 Roe Crest Drive, North Mankato, Minnesota 56003
www.mycapstone.com

Library of Congress Cataloging-in-Publication Data
Names: Golkar, Golriz, author.
Title: Bindi Irwin / by Golriz Golkar.
Description: North Mankato, Minnesota : Capstone Press, [2019] | Series:
    Influential people | Audience: Grade 4 to 6. | Includes bibliographical
    references and index.
Identifiers: LCCN 2018018712 (print) | LCCN 2018021633 (ebook) | ISBN
    9781543541724 (ebook) | ISBN 9781543541328 (hardcover : alk. paper)
Subjects: LCSH: Irwin, Bindi, 1998---Juvenile literature. | Wildlife
    conservationists--Australia--Biography--Juvenile literature.
Classification: LCC QL31.I77 (ebook) | LCC QL31.I77 G65 2019 (print) | DDC
    590.92 [B] --dc23
LC record available at https://lccn.loc.gov/2018018712

Editorial Credits
Editor: Mirella Miller
Designer: Becky Daum
Production Specialist: Ryan Gale

Quote Sources
p. 7, "Bindi Irwin Wins 'Young Conservationist of the Year' at the 27th Australian Geographic
Society Awards." *Australia Zoo*, October 30, 2014; p. 26, "Bindi Irwin." *IMDB*, n.d.

Photo Credits
AP Images: Jordan Strauss/Invision, cover; Getty Images: Bradley Kanaris/Getty Images
Entertainment, 14–15, David Livingston/Getty Images Entertainment, 27; iStockphoto: fstop123,
31; Newscom: Amanda Parks/Splash News, 24, Andrew Carlile/MEGA, 11, No Credit, 8, Snapper
Media/Splash News, 23, SUN, 19, Terry Gatanis/ZUMAPRESS, 17, United Archives/Impress/United
Archives, 12; Rex Features: Apollomovie Beteiligungs/Kobal, 20; Shutterstock Images: Featureflash
Photo Agency, 6, Kathy Hutchins, 5, 28

Design Elements: iStockphoto, Red Line Editorial, and Shutterstock Images

TABLE OF CONTENTS

CHAPTER 1

A WILDLIFE Warrior

Bindi Irwin smiled. She thanked the audience. They clapped and cheered. The year was 2014. She had just won an award. It was an award given to young people. It was given for animal **conservation**.

Irwin had helped protect animals

for years. Animals were her friends.

Irwin works to
protect animals.

5

Steve Irwin starred in many TV shows about animals.

She gave a speech. "I hope to educate and inspire as many people as I can," she said. She dedicated the award to her dad. "He was my whole world."

Irwin grew up with animals. Her parents were conservationists. Her dad, Steve, was also a famous TV star. He died when she was young. Like her dad, she wanted to teach people about animals. She wanted to protect animals. And she loved carrying on her father's work.

Irwin (right), her mother (center), and her brother (left), at a zoo event in 2017

Irwin is a busy young adult. She is a TV star. She has appeared in films. She has written books about **wildlife**. And she has won many other awards. Animals are her life. After all, she grew up at a zoo!

FAVORITE CROCODILE

Irwin's dad named her after his favorite crocodile.

CHAPTER 2

GROWING UP
at the Zoo

Irwin was born and raised in Australia.

Her parents managed the Australia Zoo.

Her family lived on the zoo grounds.

As a child, Irwin helped care for the animals. Her younger brother, Robert, helped too. They were **homeschooled**. They had lots of time to learn about animals. Irwin was not afraid of them. Her dad taught people about animals on his TV show. It was called *The Crocodile Hunter*. Irwin often joined her dad on his show.

The Irwin family's backyard was the Australia Zoo.

11

Steve Irwin and his wife, Terri, also starred in a movie, *Crocodile Hunter: Collision Course*.

A SAD ACCIDENT

Irwin starred in her own TV show at 8 years old. It was a show for kids. Her dad wanted to help her make the show.

One day, her dad had an accident. A stingray stung him. He died. It was a very sad time for the family. But Irwin was brave. She gave a speech about her dad. She said she wanted to help **endangered** animals like he had. She would continue his work.

Irwin kept her promise. She made her TV series on her own. She became a TV star herself.

Koalas and snakes were some of the animals Irwin got to play with on her TV show.

BUZZING BEES

Irwin is not afraid of most animals. But she is afraid of bees!

CHAPTER 3

BECOMING A
TV Star

Irwin's show ran for two years. She talked about animals. She rode elephants. She played with pythons. She even sang and danced! People loved her show. She won awards for it.

Irwin was the youngest person to win a Daytime Emmy Award.

Irwin was on TV often. She appeared on many shows. She talked about her work with wildlife. She even created a children's game show. It took place at her family's zoo. Kids competed in wildlife challenges. They solved animal puzzles. They ran through an **obstacle course**. It was a race to the finish!

Irwin got to play with orangutans and many other animals on her TV show.

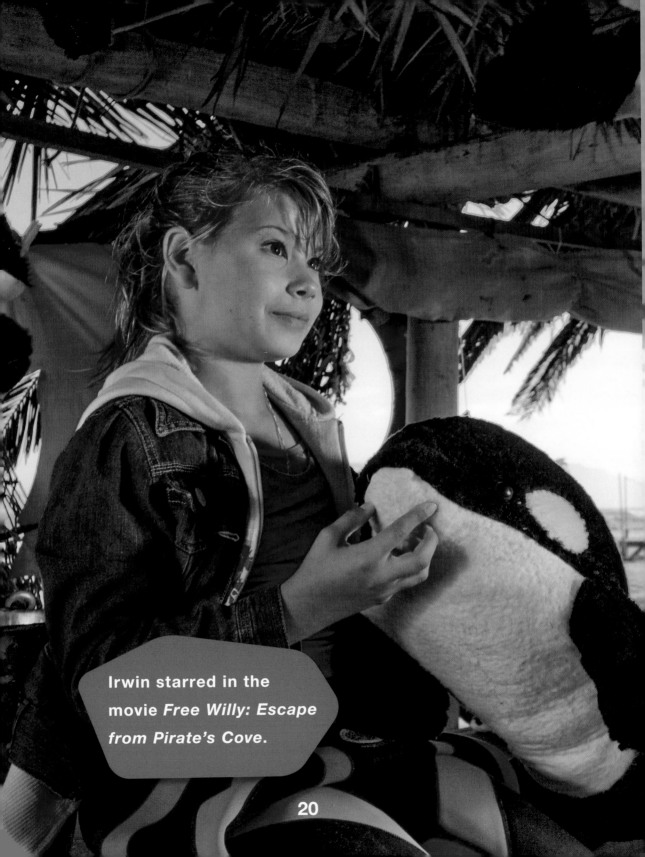

Irwin starred in the movie *Free Willy: Escape from Pirate's Cove.*

FROM TV TO MOVIES

Soon people wanted to see Irwin in movies. She appeared in a **documentary** about her dad. She filmed wildlife documentaries with her mom. Movie producers wanted her to act in their movies too. She starred in animal movies for kids. Irwin grew more popular and famous. In every movie, she showed her love for animals.

CHAPTER 4

INSPIRING
Other Kids

Irwin has done more than TV and film work. She also designs children's clothing. The clothes are made with materials that are safe for the environment. She donates the profits to wildlife programs. She also works with a wildlife **charity** her parents created. She wants to inspire kids to help animals too.

Irwin introduced her clothing line during a fashion show in 2008.

Irwin signs a copy of a book from her series, Bindi Wildlife Adventures.

Irwin is also a children's author. She wrote books about animal adventures. All along, she continued working at the Australia Zoo. She still works there today. She feeds the animals. She cuddles newborn animals. She even performs crocodile shows for visitors! With a soothing voice, she talks to the crocodiles. She also pets them. Then she feeds them a snack!

Irwin has followed her father's example. She has carried on his **legacy**. Irwin has blazed her own trail too. She inspires children through her projects. She encourages them to reach for their goals. And she has good advice for when life gets tough: "Accept the adventure!"

DANCING WITH THE STARS

In 2015, Irwin was the winner on the TV show *Dancing with the Stars!*

GLOSSARY

charity
an organization that helps people in need

conservation
protecting animals and nature from loss

documentary
a film that talks about real facts, people, and events

endangered
in danger of not existing

homeschooled
getting educated at home instead of school

legacy
ideas, values, or objects passed down from someone who lived before

obstacle course
a training area in which a person must pass through several physical challenges

wildlife
wild animals that live away from humans

TIMELINE

1998: Bindi Irwin is born in Queensland, Australia.

1998: Irwin appears on TV for the first time at 6 months old in a commercial with her dad.

2007: Irwin begins her own TV series, *Bindi the Jungle Girl*.

2008: Irwin wins the Daytime Emmy Award for Outstanding Performer in a Children's Series.

2009: With her brother, Irwin wins the "Biggest Greenies" Nickelodeon Kids' Choice Award for helping the environment.

2016: Irwin finishes an online college program and begins writing a book about her life.

ACTIVITY

ORGANIZE A CONSERVATION DAY

To keep animals safe, people need to take care of the environment. Think of some things your community could do to help our planet. Remember the old saying "Reduce, reuse, and recycle"? What materials can you use less of or use again? What can be recycled? What activities can you do to help protect the environment and reduce pollution?

Make a list of ten ideas, and share it with your friends and family. Then choose a day when everyone can get together and do as many things on the list as possible. After your conservation day, make sure to keep practicing those good habits as much as you can!

FURTHER RESOURCES

Love learning about Bindi Irwin? Learn more here:

Breguet, Amy. *Steve and Bindi Irwin.* New York: Chelsea House, 2010.

Gagne, Tammy. *Day by Day with Bindi Sue Irwin.* Hockessin, DE: Mitchell Lane, 2013.

Inside Bindi's World
http://www.holidayswithkids.com.au/feature_stories/bindi-interview

Tieck, Sarah. *Bindi Irwin.* Minneapolis, MN: Abdo, 2009.

Want to find out more about zoos and saving animals? Check these out:

Australia Zoo
http://www.australiazoo.com.au

San Diego Zoo Kids: Save Animals
http://kids.sandiegozoo.org/save-animals

INDEX